Everything Works A Little

Simple, effective Small Business Marketing

By Scott Pillsbury

Copyright © 2021 Scott Pillsbury
All Rights Reserved.
ISBN-13: 9798500620392

Dedication

This book is dedicated to all the small business owners and marketing directors out there trying to move their business forward. Building a meaningful connection with customers is very hard. It takes discipline, patience, and courage.

More importantly, it is dedicated to my amazing family who put up with my hours and efforts working on these ideas. Your support kept me moving forward and I am thankful for you.

Everything Works A Little

Acknowledgements

"If I have seen further, it is by standing on the shoulders of giants" - Sir Isaac Newton, 1675

I love this quote because it captures the basic fact that nobody ever does anything great on their own. That is certainly the case with me and this book. I have been blessed with mentors, friends and collaborators that brought me the right idea at the right time. And I am also very thankful to so many authors who gave me great ideas without ever meeting me.

Specifically, I am thankful for my sister and business partner in the printing business. She supported and backed me as I worked out these ideas in real practice in our business.

Finally, I thank every customer of Rose City Label that trusted us with their very important printing projects. Hopefully our marketing resonated with you and helped you feel connected to our business. You are the reason our business exists.

Everything Works A Little

Table of Contents

Everything Works A Little *1*
Dedication *3*
Acknowledgements *5*
Table of Contents *7*
Introduction *8*
Chapter 1 – Back to Basics *11*
Chapter 2 – Let's Get Started *19*
Chapter 3 – Setting the Foundation *30*
Chapter 4 – Do the Work *36*
Chapter 5 – Release the Brakes *47*
Chapter 6 – Go for It! *54*
Recommended Reading List *59*
About the Author *61*

Introduction

<u>Everything Works A Little</u> is a marketing philosophy, a budding consulting practice, and now it is a book, too. Thank you for your interest in learning to improve your business. This book is created for small business owners, marketing directors, and freelance entrepreneurs that want to take their business to the next level. Our aim is to attract a steady stream of highly qualified buyers that are perfectly situated to benefit from your services.

Everything Works A Little is a compilation and distillation of many high-quality business marketing books, but more importantly the method has been battle tested in my own small business for over a decade. Our suggestions don't require new software, a total brand makeover, or a huge financial investment.

The strategies are 100% actionable and they can be applied in any business setting. All industries, all sizes, all stages of business development can benefit from this method. And to be perfectly honest, there isn't much new here. We are packaging and teaching this in an engaging way with the hope of spurring action. None of the techniques are particularly complex or difficult but keeping the flywheel of marketing going does take consistent, sustained effort.

The basic premise is that if you can discover or create your unique purpose and mission, figure out what problem you solve, and for whom you solve it, then you are on the way to massive growth. Then, by asking these ideal customers where and how they want to learn from you, you can provide an ongoing stream of valuable educational content that will ultimately bring them into your customer family. That's it.

- Know yourself and why your business exists
- Know the exact personal problem you solve

- Know who can benefit most from the solution
- Based on those, determine channels and tactics

Wash, rinse, repeat. Never give up on this and you will propel your business to new heights.

Why am I such a believer? These things work. Check out the sales graph from our printing business. Once we started consistently, proactively marketing on a regular basis, things really took off. Read on and you can do the same in your business.

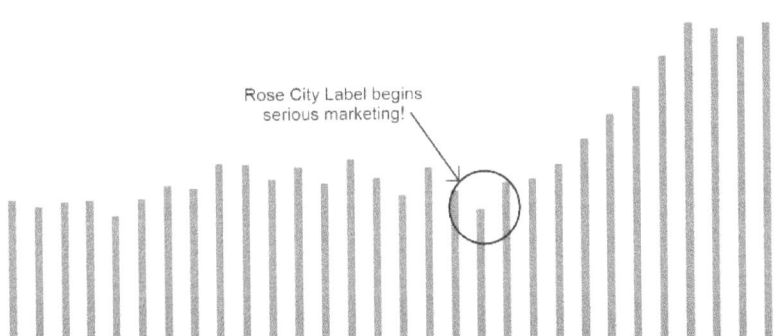

Everything Works A Little

Chapter 1 – Back to Basics

<u>What is Marketing?</u>

Marketing is the intentional act (or acts) of shaping a Brand. The BRAND is the unseen and often unknown perception of a future interaction, company, event, or product. The BRAND is the premade promise in the mind of your customer. This is the ideal that your business has to live up to in the eyes of the consumer.

Every business, person, organization, or product already has a BRAND. It is impossible to not have a brand – anything known to another person is known by the brand the carry. This may be positive or negative, strongly developed or very vague, but everything has a brand. BRAND is not the same as, but is related to, perception, reputation, and expectation about a future activity or product use. This is the good (and often bad thing) *you and your business ALREADY have a brand!* Our job as marketers is to intentionally (and honestly) craft this brand into the aspirational goal that you are trying to fulfil with your product or service.

Marketing is not an event or even a single activity or type of activity. Social media isn't marketing – it is one activity that may support marketing, but this one thing on its own is not marketing. Marketing is the sum of all activities/images/sounds/reviews over time to influence the perception of a brand in the eyes of their ideal customer.

Whether we like it or not, we and our business already have a brand. The key to marketing is to positively influence that brand perception with honest testimonials, educational content, and other relevant information that directs the ideal customer to engage with us.

Who Does Marketing Apply To?

The ideas and tactics in this book apply to any product, service, business. They even apply to an individual person. Everyone has a personal brand – and hopefully that personal brand is aligned with the brand of the organization they represent.

For the purpose of this book and easy reading, we will refer to the brand of your business, but that isn't the only organization this applies to. Your business could be a non-profit, a government agency, a club, sport, or church. These ideas and tactics could also apply to an individual product, idea, program, or offering.

Basically, anything that a person has a perception of has a brand – anything a person even knows about has a brand because, they have some type of good or bad perception of that product or business. So, anything that is known to another person is a product or business that can be helped by effective marketing.

Please don't get hung up on the very specific narrow niche you occupy – if you have any product/service/message that you are trying to communicate to another human, this book applies to you and there are lessons you can learn. You have a brand whether you intentionally craft it or not. The brand exists in the mind of your consumer – and your job is to craft that brand in a positive, authentic way to get more people to come and interact with the brand on a deeper level.

The other Side of Marketing

Marketing is the precursor to sales. Sales is the final step in the marketing continuum. The two activities are complementary. Marketing should set the table for the sales team and bring in a steady stream of qualified, interested target consumers for your product or service.

More than just the sales team, your entire business has to fulfill the promises made by marketing. Explicitly or by inference, your marketing activities set up an expectation in the mind of the consumer – and the business must fulfill or exceed those expectations. Nothing kills trust faster than unfulfilled expectations. Marketing must set realistic, achievable expectations in the mind of the target consumer.

Practice Makes Permanent

Mastery of any skill, including marketing, requires deliberate practice and effort. Nobody accidentally became great at anything. This pursuit of marketing excellence requires a decision and a commitment to put time, energy, and resources into the cause. There is an old (bad) saying that 'Practice Makes Perfect' but I totally disagree with this. Practice doesn't make perfect unless you are deliberately and repeatedly practicing in a perfect manner.

Just doing 100 bad free throws in basketball will not make you a great free throw shooter – it will cement in the physical action of shooting a basketball, but maybe you will just be solidifying a bad habit. The specific way that you dribble at the line, the bend of your knees, the gaze of your eyes toward the basket. These small details – if repeated over and over – will become ingrained in your mind and body.

Rather than just knocking out 100 repetitions, it is far better to do 50 perfect repetitions. There are true best practices – a good coach can show you the exact mechanics required to consistently make free throws. It isn't random. Yes, each person has specific physical characteristics and body type, but the basic fundamentals are timeless and all but the very elite level college athlete or beyond should be sticking to the basics.

Repeating the process will make it permanent, but not necessarily perfect. WHAT you practice matters, not just the blind repetition of bad technique.

The same is true for marketing. These are likely new activities and things you haven't previously made time for in your otherwise busy work life. Sales, administration, leadership, and many other things already have your plate full (or more than full!). Adding in marketing will take discipline and it will take time until it feels natural. This is where the practice element comes in. Even if it isn't perfect on day one, use the best practices (like we describe later in this book) and just begin to practice.

A very prolific author was asked how he generated so much content and he replied, with great humility, candor, and honesty – "200 shitty words per day – that is the goal." What he found over time is that once he was at 200 words, he was in the groove. The words just kept coming and usually he was near 1000 words written per day – but he was only (mentally) committed to writing 200.

And the quality came with time – he studied, learned from others, and took input from editors - but just showing up and doing the work mattered – especially in the beginning.

Small Differences Add Up

There are times when businesses need a massive makeover. The company needs a new name, location, logo, mission statement, color scheme and slogan. These are pivotal times in the life of a business, and they are important, but more often for readers of this book, you just need to take small consistent actions. The fear that your business requires a monumental, expensive change paralyzes many marketers and stops them from even taking the first step. This is the wrong attitude. Moving forward and taking action is often the most important thing.

A brand isn't built in a day or with one massive blow-out promotional campaign. As we discussed above, you already have a brand. Your brand exists in the mind of past customers and all prospects that currently know about your business. Our job as marketers is to gently shape and improve that brand through deliberate marketing activities.

Our approach here is to go to the gym and eat smaller portions – not gastric bypass surgery. If your business is truly in need of drastic measures to survive, this book may not be the right fit for you right now. It could help, but we are not going for full transformation in one weekend.

This book and its techniques are all about steady progress toward a worthy goal. Small actions, taken consistently over time, make a massive difference. But it isn't a quick fix.

It is also hard to see the changes from inside the business you are changing. Ask your friends – or better yet – survey your ideal target customers – and ask them their opinion, image, perception of your business and see how it changes over a 6-12-month timeframe. This time span is enough to make a meaningful difference – it may not be a massive difference, but it will be noticeable. Your small actions are compounding and building on each other. All these actions taken over time will help you to transform your business into an entirely new entity in the mind of your ideal target customer.

Strategy and Tactics

This book covers the two fundamental parts of a marketing effort. There are numerous books written about each part, but for this book we are covering both at a level of depth that allows you to take meaningful action. This isn't an academic treatise about the subject, but an actionable, real world guide to making your business better. Sustained results will take time and discipline, but you should be able to begin very soon. For that reason, we aren't diving into a detailed discussion about nuance and history but getting right to the nuggets of wisdom that allow you to begin taking meaningful action. With that said, it is important to have a backdrop and perspective on Strategy and Tactics.

Sadly, these words are often used interchangeably but they are not interchangeable at all. These are both important concepts, but they are more like the two sides of one coin. They work together and co-exist, but they are not the same. Neither can survive and thrive without the other.

Strategy is the big picture – the vision of where we are going. It should have some level of detail that offers clarity, but not be so focused or detailed that it requires frequent updating. Strategy is technically a level down from vision, but it is much closer to vison than tactics. Examples:

VISION – to be the finest vision care provider in Northeast Portland

STRATEGY – by using the latest technology and having the newest eyewear styles, our customers will have outstanding eye health and strong fashion sense when they leave our luxurious clinic

In this case the vision is very broad – it could almost apply to any eye clinic that is trying to be successful. The strategy, on the other hand, is very specific. It tells how you are going to live out that vision. It is very clear that this isn't the low-price leader, they don't specifically cater to children or focus on complex, rare eye disease. Defining what you are NOT is almost as important as what you are. You must have boundaries that define the edges of your 'lane' on the business success superhighway.

Taking this down to the ground level even further, we assemble a set of TACTICS that allow us to live out this strategy. There are often many different tactics that are used – sometimes all at one time and sometimes in a cyclical fashion – to enact the strategy and become the vision of your business you aspire to. In this example, relevant TACTICS could be:

TACTICS – clean, well-lit location. Comfortable waiting room with coffee, tea, soft music. Ongoing investment in diagnostic technology. Extensive certifications by doctors. Frequently updated eyewear choices. Ongoing social media marketing. iPad kiosk for check in, billing verification. Image based social media (Instagram) to show beautiful people with fashion eyewear. 'Club' mentality – referral incentives and loyalty points for being a part of the 'tribe.'

Chapter 1 – Back to Basics
Summary and Notes

Your Brand is the image and expectation that has been created in the mind of your target consumer. Every business, agency, or person has a Brand, whether they build it intentionally or not.

Marketing is the sum of all the activities that create an impression in the mind of your target customer. These are conscious, purposeful actions done by you, as well as all the other actions and interactions people have with your business. Your job as a marketer, is to craft that marketing message to bring in the right number of highly qualified, perfectly targeted prospects.

You need to take small, consistent actions to build your Brand with the right marketing activities. It isn't hard, but it does take discipline to stick with it until you see results.

NOTES:

_____
_____
_____
_____
_____
_____
_____
_____
_____
_____

Chapter 2 – Let's Get Started

Know Yourself

Knowing yourself is the beginning of building an authentic business. You – and in this case we are referring to 'You' the business – need to have a crystal-clear vision of who you are and why you exist. If you can't articulate the exact personality and character of your business, you won't be able to properly communicate it to your ideal target customer. Just like people, businesses have a personality – they have a specific vibe or feeling associated with them. If you have a physical retail location where customers meet you, this space will have a certain décor and flavor. If you are online and connected via advertising, then the visual images in your display ads, billboards, and vehicles will carry a message. If you communicate via email, text, or social media messages, the tone and voice of these messages is a big part of your identity.

Again – as we said before – your business HAS a personality and a brand. Our job as marketers is to authentically represent that in a consistent, honest way. We want to proactively and intentionally craft, curate and share this brand image with our ideal target market when they are ready to buy our products and services – this is the holy grail of marketing success – right message, delivered to the right audience, at the right time.

A precursor to any of this is knowing yourself and your true nature/brand/essence.

If you are a solo entrepreneur, this is a bit easier to distill because for better or worse, your individual personality is the business. YOU are the business in the mind of your customers. Even if the business name is Alpha Services, the consumer sees, "my friend Bob Johnston the plumber." You are the brand.

If you have a team or larger organization, and a physical location, then it is more complex because the business brand and personality is a compilation of all these sensory touch points that your clients experience. Every aspect of your business – from answering the phone to sending the invoice – is a building block on the brand experience for your customer. Be intentional about EVERY aspect of this customer interaction. Unfortunately, the consumer is likely to remember (and complain about) the one person or aspect of the business that wasn't up to par much more than they will the other four touch points that went well.

Be consistent – one of the red flags in the consumer mind that breaks trust and confidence is a lack of consistency. Even if two different departments are both very good, it is a red flag if they are different. You can't staff your business with robots or expect people to all read from exactly the same script with the same tone and inflection in their voice, but you can try to build a consistent culture that aligns with your brand.

So, what is that brand voice – and who are YOU as a business? There aren't necessarily wrong answers to this question, but you will be most successful if you thoughtfully and intentionally set this direction in advance. The example of a restaurant or bar is instructive since most all of us have experienced service in a place like this. What is your restaurant trying to be?

Comfort food and warm environment? Or latest trendy small bites and sharp angles?
Do you rotate the menu frequently with experimental items? Or steady, consistent fare?
What is the price point?

Family friendly? Or more of a date night place?
Dress code? Or peanut shells on the floor and loud music?
Laminated plastic menu? Or iPad on each table?
Table service with uniformed staff? Or order at the bar and bus your table?

None of these options are bad. Any of these characteristics could be elements of a very successful business. What we are trying to discover, or design, is the most authentic presentation of your business. Yes, this is a group effort based on the collective 'vibe' of all your staff and perhaps multiple owners, but for the purpose of this exercise, there has to be one leader/founder that is the true burning fire behind the idea.

We are trying to live out this one person's best vision of themselves in the form of a business.

So, part one of this section is to truly discover (or design) this brand personality for the business in as much detail as possible. Part two is to execute the vision at all levels so that every interaction, marketing presentation, ad and image is 100% consistent. Nobody feels good about going to a Country bar with Heavy Metal music playing. Even if it is a welcome change on that day, there will be an underlying confusion in the customers' mind, and it will leave a negative impression of your business.

With careful marketing and alignment, we can keep everything consistent and exceed all customer expectations. This leads to happy repeat customers that refer our business to others.

The Problem You Solve

Once you have a clear vision of yourself – the company and person you want to be when you are fully living into your life's purpose – then you can begin to move out into the world. Having this core, baseline understanding of your own strengths and values helps you answer the next question – *what problem do we solve?*

This is critical and takes some time to figure out. Regardless of whether you are selling a physical product, an online course, or a service sold by the hour, nobody wants what you are selling. Nobody! What they want is the RESULT your product provides. They want the transformational feeling that your product or service provides.

Usually, in the case of B2B (business to business – selling to other businesses) offerings, your product must RESULT in lower cost, higher revenue, or less risk/uncertainty. In the case of B2C (business to consumer – selling to individuals for personal use) sales, these same feelings translate into less pain, greater pleasure, or less risk/hassle. The motivations for a business purchase aren't the same as a personal one, but they are related. At the end of the day, in nearly all cases, it is a person that is actually placing the order with you, and we all have human motivations and fears.

So, to really tap into the visceral need that will excite your ideal customer, you need to be laser focused on the problem you solve. The specific product features, the sizing, the fabric, the colors, and even the pricing will all flow from this understanding of the problem being solved. If you can dig into the core motivation and feeling that will make a person purchase, then all these details fall into place rather easily.

To continue this apparel example, your focus is very different for a shirt you create for men that makes them feel bold and strong, versus a dress for women that makes them feel slim and delicate. Both products are clothing – both made from cloth and maybe selling for the same price point in the market – but the feeling you are trying to engender in the person wearing the garment is much different. As a result, the design, the sales pitch, the advertising – all of these are targeted toward the feeling you are creating within the buyer.

This feeling isn't just created by the product itself – it begins with the brand. The feeling of the brand and the reputation/association a person feels by wearing certain name-brand products is just as important as the fit and comfort of the actual product. People wear branded shirts for many reasons, and only one of the (minor) reasons is how well the shirt fits. People wear 'Air Jordan' basketball clothing because they want to be associated with MJ, #23, the greatest of all time (GOAT), not because they have no other clothes to wear.

They want the feeling and the confidence they feel when they look in the mirror and see themselves connected to this larger brand. This is equally true of high fashion products, cause-based products that support education, charitable causes, or environmental charities. All these surrounding aspects – as much or more than the physical product – are related to the purchase decision in the mind of the buyer.

What is the problem we are solving? Once you figure that out – and the end feeling your customer should feel when they interact with your brand, product, or business – you are on your way to designing an offering that resonates with your ideal target consumer. If this is done well, and there is a true connection made, the product should sell itself.

Know Your IDEAL Customer

Knowing yourself and the problem you are uniquely qualified to solve is only a part of the way to the finish line. You need to know *for whom* you solve this problem. The solution you are providing doesn't exist in a vacuum – it must be tailored to the particular person you are trying to help.

Even with your own gifts and talents well documented, and the specific pain you are trying to alleviate (or pleasure you are trying to create), there is still a big, wide open set of people you could be helping. And, just to clarify, even if you are a B2B service provider or company, you are still solving problems for and selling your services to, people.

A business never purchased anything – a person within a business is the buyer. Yes, there are differences – selling weight loss products to a person for their personal use is different than selling software to a business, but the human (or humans) responsible for the purchase still must be reached at a deep level. Not saying these buyers on the software committee aren't professional and focused on the needs of their organization, but they are still people. We all make emotional decisions and then find the data to confirm our initial (emotional) decision, so it looks good on the decision matrix.

WHO you sell to is critical. Being too broad and trying to capture a larger market is a recipe for disaster. Generalist companies are poor companies. Our objective here is to narrow your focus and then take that result and cut it in half. The more specific and narrow your market can be, the better you will connect.

The ideal customer should experience your company like they are coming home to a family dinner or attending a college reunion. It should just feel right – they should feel like they belong, and they are among friends. People want to belong – they want to feel 'normal' when they seek services or products. If everyone in the waiting room of your clinic is 'like' them, they will LIKE you. This similarity could take many forms:

- Same age
- Same gender
- Same broken foot
- Same skin rash
- Same small dog with a cold

Whatever these similar characteristics are, they will connect your potential customers to future customers. Everyone wants to be in a tribe – they want to belong with their people. We use the example of patients (or parents/owners of patients) in the waiting room because it is a very visual, common example. Even if your business doesn't have a waiting room or even a physical location, the feeling is the same. Regardless of how people interact with your business, it should draw them in like a magnet.

The Red Velvet Rope – Cut the Market Again

In his wonderful book, Book Yourself Solid, author Michael Port talks about a very important concept – the Red Velvet Rope. The metaphor uses the waiting line at a very popular concert or club. There is a line out the door and around the block to get into the event. There are security guards walking around with walkie talkie radios to stay in constant communication. The crowd is queued up in lines, weaving back and forth on the sidewalk. The lines are kept in order by a series of red velvet ropes on chrome posts. The red velvet rope keeps order and assures that everyone is in the proper position in line. Then, just as you are shuffling up slowly in line, another person walks up and bypasses the entire process.

The most valuable, welcome guest goes right to the front of the line – with no waiting or shuffling. This person is a VIP – a very important person. They are invited inside the red velvet rope – with direct access to the show. This is the way you want your ideal clients to feel – they are a very special, select group that *get* to work with you directly. It is a privilege that many seek but few are granted.

Your business will still happily serve the other people waiting in line. They deserve your service too, but they *only* get access to your products and services after the most valuable, hand-picked VIP guests are served.

This isn't an elitist, arrogant way to think about your business. Rather, it recognizes the scarcity of your time and attention. Time is the most precious and limited resource we have. By definition, you can't serve everyone. There is a finite amount of 'you' to go around. Even with a large team, there is still a limit to the people you can reach with your message, product, or service. With that in mind, you need to be very careful about how you allocate this limited resource. If, as with most successful businesses, you truly feel that you are helping people with your business, then you owe it to the clients and to yourself to focus on the people that need you the most.

It is a form of triage – or sorting – to prioritize and limit your focus to the people or businesses that you can help the most. This is a service to the clients. Spending (or wasting) your time on customers that won't get maximum benefit from the work you do is wasteful and foolish.

So, when in doubt, cut your target market rather than expanding it. If you are in startup mode trying to pay the basic bills, it will be scary to turn down anyone with a pulse and a wallet. That is understandable, but it is also a sign that you are on the right path. By serving the people that you are truly called to serve, you will be living at your highest professional level.

Working with the ideal clients (not just any client) will energize and motivate you. As you solve their unique and important problems, you will be rewarded in your heart not just your bank account. These people are the ones that make it exciting to get out of bed in the morning. This is why you went to culinary school, dental school, business school in the first place. These are the people you were thinking about serving as an apprentice doing the grunt work to learn your craft. No, not every client in your business will feel like this, but you must aim for these people and maximize your time with them. You will be personally fulfilled, and your business will grow and thrive in the process.

<u>What about the Others?</u>

The 'others'- those outside of your target market – will still come. Nobody is suggesting a moratorium on people that aren't a perfect fit. Rather, it is the focus you place on attracting the ideal target customer. This is the ideal – but nothing ever goes 100% according to plan. Think of it as a target in archery, with concentric rings around the bullseye. We would like to serve only the people in the true center of the target, but in reality, we may move out to the next two or three rings. Until our business is so popular and sought after that we can truly book all our capacity with ideal, bullseye customers, we will need to move out to the next rings enough to fill our time/machine/restaurant.

The important thing here is focus. Who are you speaking to and how are you reaching them? If you truly live for the opportunity to create financial plans for divorced women in their 40's and beyond, then by all means target them. Speak directly to their issues – college planning, retirement, medical care, and health. Be specific and show them that you know how to solve their specific problems. Not general, academic problems, but their specific problems.

By targeting and speaking directly to your target market, you will not alienate the adjacent markets (older or younger women, divorced men, married women). They will still come! Often, they will be referred by a person that is in your target group because of the excellent service you provide. These are still good and valuable clients – people you can serve and truly help – but they aren't the ideal you are searching for. Working with them takes a bit more time, doesn't feel as good, and perhaps isn't as profitable. That's OK. They are in the next few outer rings from the bullseye.

"No Thank You" Prospects

Continuing the metaphor of the archery target, you also must realize that there are people in the outer rings of the target or even those that represent arrows that miss the target and the hay bale altogether. There are some people that you must politely say, "No Thank You" to when they contact you for service. Just like a restaurant with the sign that says. "We reserve the right to refuse service to anyone", you need to reserve this right as well. People may be excluded for many reasons, and as long as they aren't discriminatory, mean or illegal reasons, feel free to set your boundaries any way you choose.

Some clients are so difficult to work with that they will never be profitable. They may be personally hard to communicate with, they may not be able to pay your price, or they may have a particular problem that you can't solve.

Don't waste time with these people. Instead, have a ready list of competitors that may be able to serve them better. Refer them with a smile and let them know you wish them the best success in the future. If something changes with their needs or specific profile, and they fit within your bullseye in the future, you would be happy to have them back. This is the best, most authentic solution for your business and the client.

Chapter 2 – Let's Get Started
Summary and Notes

Having a successful business with an authentic brand begins with knowing yourself. By yourself, I mean *you* the business. The business has a distinct personality, history, and vision for the future. Knowing exactly who you are is vital.

Next, you need to know the problem you solve. Why would someone come to you? How do you help them? How do you make the lives of your buyers better? You must know exactly the problem you solve so you can share it with the target audience.

Finally, when you know who you are and the problem you solve, you need to figure out who you solve that problem for. Who are you helping? Don't be a generalist – be very narrow and target your ideal, perfect customer.

NOTES:

Chapter 3 – Setting the Foundation

<u>Slowly Adjust your Products and Services</u>

Now that the basic concepts are understood, we are ready to dive in and begin work. There are two specific things you can focus on, but since you can't do everything at once, you need to be strategic and what I call, "aggressively patient". Now that you know yourself and your business vision, the problem you solve, and the people or businesses you serve, you need to craft your product or service. Depending on your stage of business development, you may be just starting out and creating your first products, or intentionally retooling an existing business. In either case, now is the time to align your offerings (the actual things people pay you for) with your newly clarified brand mission.

Again, if you are starting up or starting over, you almost have an advantage – you have a blank canvas to create your vision on. If, however, you are buying an existing business or just updating and improving a business you already own or manage, you need to respect the heritage. You need to build on past success. Something must have been working, or the business wouldn't have survived at all. Business is tough! It is quite an accomplishment just to survive your first 5 years in business. Don't throw that away, but rather slowly edge your enterprise toward your new vision.

In most cases, there is no need to fully and abruptly throw out everything you have done. You can slowly adjust your offerings, your marketing, your products over time if it is done with intention. Yes, you may have to make a hard break at some point when you are fully getting out of the life insurance business and fully focusing on long term care and wealth management – that is possible. But don't throw away all your existing business until you have built up that new business to take its place. You still need to eat. The business still must survive and profitably provide a paycheck to you and your team.

You can responsibly and methodically adjust your product offerings to align with your new direction, but you don't have to blow up your existing business to make that happen. Besides adjusting the product offerings, you also need to gently adjust your marketing and brand message to bring your new vision to life.

Marketing to your Mission

Besides adjusting your product offering in a more intentional way, your marketing needs to be adjusted too. That is the primary focus of this book, but it must be adjusted and aligned in combination with the actual products and services you offer to the customers. Product development and product marketing must work very closely together. They don't exist in isolation. Everything must be aligned to have a positive, synergistic, growing business.

Marketing or product? This was the subject of a seminar I attended years ago. They had a graph with four quadrants. On one axis was product quality. On the other was marketing quality and effectiveness. There are four possible options:

Great product – bad marketing – best kept secret, lucky to be alive
Bad product – great marketing – snake oil, dishonest
Great product – great marketing -- holy grail, massive success
Bad product – bad marketing – dead man walking, soon to be closed

We recognize that you can't do everything at once. Perhaps you are working in a large organization and only have control of a small portion of the overall company direction. In this case, you need to temper your expectations and do the best you can within your domain. There is great honor in making your department the best it can be. But for OUR ideal customers (readers) we are talking to small business owners, marketing directors, VP of Operations – people that can pull the levers to make change. For those people, the question is, how do you allocate your precious, limited time, energy, and budget? Do you work on the product development, or the marketing?

Every business is different, so we can't really give a blanket answer for all situations. Your product must be solid or even very good to have something worthy of marketing. See option #2 above – nobody wants to 'trick' people into buying a poor product – that is dishonest, unsatisfying, and often immoral. That is not our goal with this book. But often the case is reversed. The product *is* good enough, but the marketing is so poor, the business is stagnant or even going backwards.

In many cases, the founder/owner came up through the ranks as a technical expert. They started a plumbing company because they were a journeyman plumber and wanted to control their destiny. Or they were an IT expert, so they build a business around their passion or hobby. Whatever the background, it is often easier for us to dig into the technical details trying to make the actual product 3% better. That is a mistake – and a disservice to the people you serve. Your ideal target clients probably *aren't* journeyman plumbers or IT experts. They need excellent quality products and services, but you probably already offer that, and tweaking the small details is really a form of procrastination.

If you are a mission-driven business and leader, you should believe deep in your heart that you are helping people. Some would almost call your business a calling or a ministry. You are uniquely qualified and called to help your target customers with your specific product or service. If that is the case – if you are really on a mission to help people – then you need to put serious effort into reaching those ideal target people. To deprive them of your outstanding service would be selfish. It is not fair to let those ideal, bullseye customers work with the *second-best option* for their insurance, plumbing, or whatever you provide to make their lives better.

Yes, you need to constantly evolve and improve. Yes, you should be better at your craft next year than you are this year, but don't let that refinement get in the way of marketing your amazing products today.

Focus and Distill your Brand Promise

Now that you know yourself, your ideal client, and the problem you solve, you are ready to begin. The last thing you need is a distilled, concise message – your Unique Selling Proposition (USP). Your entire brand ethos is complex, but you need to be able to boil it down to a single sentence. You can't condense a complex business with a rich heritage into a sound bite, and that is not the goal. Rather, the focus of the USP is the 'U' – the unique thing that you bring to the table. What makes you different and better than every other business in your category? If you are just 'me too auto repair', you will have a miserable, short, unprofitable business life. Something must set you apart. What is it?

You can't and shouldn't avoid competition. Competition makes us all stronger. But, to win, you need a very specific reason for people to choose you. If you are a dentist, there may be 50 dental offices in your city. Why choose you? What makes you unique or special – this must be a fact or a supportable number. Just saying 'we try harder' doesn't cut it. Here is a great formula for this that a friend shared with me years ago:

- Who we help?
- What we help them feel or achieve?
- By offering what product or service?

- In what unique way?

In the case of my company, Rose City Label, we have a very clear USP. It defines who we serve, the problem we solve (or feeling we create), what we offer to achieve that, and the UNIQUE and special way we do it.

We help Pacific Northwest food, beverage, and product companies
Build their brand connection with their customers and grow their business
By providing excellent quality printed labels, delivered on time, at a fair price
Backed by the most experienced, eco-friendly family-owned printing company in the area

Or, more simply.

We help PNW companies grow and connect with their customers by providing high quality product labels backed by an outstanding company.

This isn't a final product that will never change, but this general spirit has been the same for most of our 94-year history. It has certainly been the same for the 27 years I have been in the business. The products, services, and technologies change, but the core – The Unique Selling Proposition – should be solid and basically unwavering. Once you have all this information in your toolkit, it is time to put these ideas into action.

Chapter 3 – Setting the Foundation
Summary and Notes

Maybe you are a start up and you can create all this before you even open your doors. Or, more likely, you are an established business trying to pivot and be more intentional. In either case, you need to distill your brand consciously and intentionally.

You need to clearly state the problem you solve, for whom, why they should choose *you* among all other options.

This is your Unique Selling Proposition (USP). It is the clear, bright light that all your marketing efforts point people toward.

NOTES:

Chapter 4 – Do the Work

<u>Armed and Dangerous</u>

Now that you have all this background taken care of, you are ready to begin systematically and strategically telling your authentic brand story to the right people. This is the next step, telling the true, authentic story to the *right* potential target (bullseye) customers in just the right format for them. This is critical – you must carefully and thoughtfully craft the message and select your personal tribe you are called to serve – but then you have to reach them *where and how they want to be reached*. We will go through some specific tools below, but these tools may be obsolete within a year.

Some have a longer shelf life, but several of the tools (especially specific technology platforms) can rotate out of favor very quickly. We will use some specific tools as examples, but this book is not designed to provide a 'how to' guide for any specific tool. Our mission is all about the mindset and the overarching brand message being delivered.

The message is no good if it isn't delivered. Delivery and reception by your ideal target customer are the desired results. A great ad, logo, or tagline is useless if they aren't consumed by the right people. The question is, "Where/how does my target market want to consume my brand story so that it will most effectively influence them to call me when they need my services?" How do you learn this? Two simple ways – market research and asking your current best clients.

Market Research Doesn't have to be Scientific

You probably already have a good idea of where to reach your best clients. You may have already connected with them individually through these channels, but now you want to take this outreach and connection to the next level. Where do your people live? What conferences do they attend? What social media do they participate in, if any? What publications do they read? Who do they trust as influencers within their field?

In very broad strokes, you can probably make a guess about where to find more people like your best customers. But if you have the courage, you could just ask! Current clients would be flattered if you asked them, "Bob, you are really a perfect fit for our business. We enjoy working with you and feel like you get tremendous value from our program – you always give us great testimonials, right? Our business would really thrive if we could find 5 or 10 more top level clients like you – the more like you, the better! If I was looking to help more people just like you, Bob, where should I find them?"

This is a bit of an open-ended question, so you probably want to prepare Bob for the question – let him know a week ahead of time when you are confirming your quarterly account review that you will be asking him this question. Besides preparing him in advance, give him some good ideas based on our (unscientific) market research above – "Bob, we have had good luck finding client at the quarterly ABC conference, advertising in the widget trade journal, and by offering weekly educational content on our Facebook page.

Do those seem like the right locations to you? If you didn't know us already, where would you look for someone providing our type of service?" Then, just listen and take notes. This is pure gold! A respected, valuable client in the center of your bullseye telling you where people like him hang out. Now you just have to execute.

Small, Steady, Consistent

Nothing worthwhile is built quickly. It takes time to become a trusted expert in the mind of your ideal customer. It can be overwhelming to think of all the *possible* things you could do. As a small business owner or marketing leader, there literally is no end to the job. There are always more ways to reach out, better content to write, and more people to help. It is never ending, and that can stop you from even beginning. Don't let that happen. Just start. Thankfully, you don't have to start by random luck – your very valuable and ideal client has already given you a few good ideas of where people like him hang out. Start there.

As we mentioned before, the specific tactics can change over time. Platforms, rules, and electronic algorithms could render very specific tactical advice obsolete before you ever find this book, so we won't get caught in that trap. Below are general suggestions and recommendations for the broad categories of marketing outreach. Your mileage may vary, so please try something, be patient and consistent, but evaluate and be ready to pivot over time.

Social media. This is the hottest thing to happen to marketing in decades. It is 'free', easy to use, and the audience keeps growing. BUT, because of all those reasons it is very hard to stand out or be memorable on these platforms. And always remember, you are building your house on rented land. At any time, the owner (Facebook, IG, Tik Tok) could change the rules without warning. You have no control over the look of the platform, the reach of your posts, or even if you will be banned from the service for some random violation of a platform rule.

Social media is amazing and powerful, but it needs to feed people to your own platform or email list or physical store as quickly as possible. Then you have more direct control and contact. Use social media to your benefit (because the platform is certainly using you) but be wary of too much concentration. And this will be repeated for other channels, but *please be interesting, memorable, and valuable!* Just because the platform is free to use, the creation of good content is not easy or free. Your creative expression, and value packed content that shows you as an expert in your field is the thing that will set you apart in any channel, and especially on social media. Give away free content that people would likely pay for.

Web site. Your personal (business) website has the opposite problem from Social Media. You own it 100% and have full control, but you don't have a built-in source of traffic. You must work and claw to get people to put their eyeballs on your site. Hopefully, however, once they get there, they will stick because of your amazing, engaging, valuable content. Keep your website fresh and active with frequent updates, blog content, and useful information. You can give away a white paper, e-book, or PDF to entice visitors to give up their email address, but don't push this too hard. They may just be checking out options at this point. Be professional and informative. Give them a reason to trust you and your expertise. Then, when they need a car, gutter cleaning, or a new home, they will think of you.

Email marketing. 50 email list subscribers are probably more valuable than 500 social media followers. People that come to your website, download a free PDF, and give up their email address…those people are much more committed to you than a random like on social media. These people are voluntarily giving you access to a sacred space – their email inbox! And they are giving you access to their mind and spending some of their very limited attention on you. Don't take that for granted, but instead treat that invitation with utmost respect. Only provide them high quality, relevant content that helps them. Along the way, you will reinforce their impression of you as a professional expert in your field. When the time is right, you will be the logical choice to solve their problem. Be patient, be diligent, and you will be rewarded.

Print Ads. People have been predicting the demise of physical printing for more than a decade, but it is still going strong. The formats have changed, but depending on your audience, advertising in the right trade journal could be the ideal way to reach them. And, if you can provide editorial/educational content to the publication, that is even better. The main idea is that you want your name, business name, logo, and message to be in their field of view as often as possible. We also want them to see you in a positive, professional light. We have done this in the printing business for years. By providing free articles, and advertising in a very small, focused newsletter/magazine for the craft brewing industry, we are automatically considered industry experts. The fact that the editor of the publication ran *our* story about labels automatically shows us to be credible, vetted, trustworthy industry experts. Print ads can work, and when combined with articles submitted to the same publication, you are set up as an expert in the mind of your potential bullseye customer.

Trade Shows. Like print ads, many people think that in-person trade shows are dead. I couldn't disagree more! All industries have some type of annual or semiannual events. These are valuable as a networking opportunity for the vendors that are trying to sell to the primary attendees, but also very valuable for the people visiting the show. Being able to see all vendors in one location, catching up with old suppliers and meeting new ones, and seeing the latest products and systems for your business – these are all very valuable reasons why trade shows are far from dead. More importantly, it is a chance to socialize with peers, problem solve about broad industry issues, serve on a committee to give back to your industry, and just catch up with old friends. Online events have been better than expected recently, but nothing takes the place of in person meetings and human connection.

Personal Sales Calls. Please don't underestimate the value of a handshake. This is a bit old school, but it is real. The personal connection made with an in-person meeting can't be replicated on

Zoom, social media, or via other electronic means. There is something valuable – both for you, the service provider, and the buyer about a genuine, in person meeting. Yes, there are limitations on geography, time, and ultimately an upward limit on how many people you can serve in person, but this should still be part of your marketing. More than anything, you should do this because it is counter-cultural!

Nobody does this anymore, so if you want to stand out, visit your local customers in person – that will make an impression. What do you get in an in-person call? Only the other 90% of information that is *lost* on electronic communication. The nuance, the flavor, and the vibe of your customer is totally sanitized out of electronic communication. Personal contact brings that back. You can't drive 50 miles in our SUV for a low value prospect, but you can make strategic efforts to connect with your most important, bullseye clients, in person.

Phone is not dead! Don't discount the value of picking up the phone and saying hello! Like the personal sales call above, a phone call is (sadly) counter cultural. Most sales reps at your competitors would prefer to send an email. They worry, "what if they answer the phone?" Instead, you should be armed and ready to engage in meaningful conversation, to connect on a human level, and to be ready to cross-sell, upsell, and provide massive value to your potential clients.

The phone time is golden. The chance to personally engage a prospect, away from social media and other people vying for his or her attention is huge. Use this time wisely and strategically. Make a personal connection, but also drop value bombs and give them a reason to remember you. Your expertise and value will stay with them long after the call concludes.

Partnering and Co-promotions. If you are a successful business, you have a very valuable 'rolodex' of client contact information. Your allies have the same. (For the young people, a 'rolodex' was a physical business card file that contained all the golden contact information for your trusted resources, vendors, and clients). If you have a trusted partner that serves the same general client list, you can both benefit from doing a cross-promotion.

If I send your information about winterizing your home to my list, and you send my information about yard service to your list, we both win. And, more importantly, the clients win. They get the best vendor for winterization as they prepare for the cold months, and the best vendor for outdoor living during the warm months. The clients win, and that is good for both businesses. Find trusted partners that align on business principles and values and share information freely. This is known as 'borrowing credibility' and it is a powerful strategy if you choose your partners carefully.

Networking Groups and Events. This is more hit and miss, but you can make valuable connections if you are smart. Like social media, the barrier to entry at most networking events is low. Anyone can show up, and it is incumbent on you to vet and validate the people you want to invest in. But, with that caveat in mind, there is massive opportunity in networking. Sometimes people you connect with in totally unrelated industries can be a conduit to business opportunity.

New connections come from unlikely sources. The insurance agent you meet could introduce you to your best landscape architecture client. People that are out hustling, with reputable products and services, are huge potential sources of introductions and valuable leads. The key is mutuality. You must *give* before you *get*. This can be scary, and it takes a leap of faith, but it can pay massive dividends if done well. Commit 6-12 months to a networking group – give before you expect to get – and wait to see the multiplied results that come back to you.

Tactics and Strategy – Remember the Difference

It is critical to remember that the specific tactics and channels are just pieces of the puzzle. These things can adjust and change over time as the market dictates. Your overall guiding mission and purpose don't change. Be mindful of the difference. Keep a firm handle on your general direction and mission. Keep the people you serve in mind, and the problems you solve very clearly in your mind. But please don't get married to any specific tactic or program.

Social media platforms come and go. Your ideal bullseye customer demographic may change, or the methods to connect with them may change as their industry evolves. Tactical changes are fine, but don't let your primary strategy and mission change. Some things should be timeless, and others change with the market. Your challenge is to discern which things fit into which category. Be sure to consider this carefully before you abandon a new campaign too quickly. By the same token, don't be married to a losing strategy because of some nostalgia or misplaced loyalty. Results matter.

Follow your tribe and find them where they want to be found. Everything Works a Little – that is our mantra for a reason. There is no 'killer app' or magic bullet. There is only hard work, consistent service to the customer, and telling the truth in the most favorable way possible – also known as marketing.

Start Now, Repeat Tomorrow

Armed with this information, the biggest danger to your marketing journey is fear and hesitation. Don't let perfection be the enemy of action. Tennis great Arthur Ashe said, "Start where you are, use what you have, do what you can." This was a powerful statement that we can all learn from. Don't wait until the script is perfect, make the call. Don't hesitate on the lighting, take the picture and post it. Don't be afraid of lacking perfect information, get out of your car and knock on the door in front of you.

Perfection is the enemy of progress. Waiting for the perfect opportunity makes cowards of all salespeople. In any great endeavor there is risk. If you wait for perfect information, you will be a spectator in the game of life. Instead, get out of the gate early and get feedback. Don't be reckless but err on the side of action. If your small business is like most, there has been *exactly zero* coordinated, intelligent marketing.

Whatever you do – no matter how bad – will be better than sitting on the sidelines. Start today. Pick one tactic and implement it. Don't study it and take a poll and wait for feedback. Act. Move. Step into the action and send an email blast. Whatever the appropriate first step is, take it boldly and without apology.

Act today, and then you will have momentum. Repeat that action tomorrow. After 30 days, adjust slightly, but keep moving forward. Don't quit telling your amazing bullseye customers all the great things you can do to SERVE them. You are all about finding and attracting people you can SERVE. Don't be shy about shouting your value from the mountaintops because you are truly helping people.

Start with small, sustainable steps. Don't commit to posting on 4 different platforms daily, plus an email newsletter, plus a website update each week. That is a disaster. Start with something sustainable and build on that. One post per week on one channel. 10 sales calls per week to lapsed customers.

These are new activities that must find their way onto your already-full calendar, right? So, consider that when you are mentally or verbally committing to new tasks.

Doing ONE thing with consistency and excellence is far better than doing five things in a haphazard, once-in-a-while basis. Pick something you can commit to and be excited about and execute that with passion and excellence. That one weekly blog post will make a massive difference over time. It will be much better than an on again, off again effort to support multiple channels with video, blog content, and clever memes.

Start small, repeat with consistency, and never give up on sharing the value of your business.

Chapter 4 – Do the Work
Summary and Notes

Now that you have a basic framework to build on, it is time to do the work. Nothing that I have done or know how to suggest is very difficult. These are not sophisticated algorithms for marketing automation – these are simple, basic, effective suggestions.

Simple doesn't mean easy! The magic is in the repetition and consistency.

Just like going to the gym – you won't see results on the first day, or even the first month. Over time, with consistent focused action you will see amazing results if you stick with it. Consistency is the key more than any specific epic day of marketing.

NOTES:
_____
_____
_____
_____
_____
_____
_____
_____
_____
_____
_____

Chapter 5 – Release the Brakes

<u>Make a Commitment and Stick with It</u>

Now, it is all about execution. Don't let perfection be the enemy of progress. There will always be more research to do, always more tweaks to the blog post, and always a slightly better image for Instagram. *Those are excuses to hold you back!* Don't fall victim to this perfectionist mindset – it is deadly. Especially if taking an active role in consistent marketing is new, it will seem intimidating. You will find reasons to delay or deal with other 'important' issues. Consistent marketing activity is what author Stephen Covey calls, 'Quadrant 2 activities.' They are important but not urgent.

Marketing is like starting a fitness program – it really sucks at the beginning, but in 90 days you will be very proud of your accomplishment. The early rewards are small and infrequent. It is hard to see progress.

Therefore, you need to COMMIT to a reasonable, sustainable schedule and then just do it. Don't commit to more than you can sustain; when in doubt, set the bar lower than you think it should be, so you have absolutely no excuse to skip your committed weekly activity. When I started on this journey 10 years ago, I committed to one decent blog post per week. Then, once each quarter I took the best of those 12 blog posts and sent an email blast. That was it – two things – weekly blog post and quarterly email. I didn't commit to anything else. I didn't write 52 blog posts per year, but I got 45-48 per year for several years.

That consistent writing showed our visitors that we are label printing experts. We showed examples of our work, gave technical advice, and gave a peek inside our company with employee projects, holiday parties, and recycling efforts. This commitment and consistency aren't the only thing that helped our business – remember that 'Everything Works A Little.' We also had outside sales, referrals, and continuous improvement in print quality. All those things together working in a virtuous cycle allowed us to double our business in 10 years.

Make a commitment that you can stick with. Create some content today, and then repeat on your schedule. Look at the results in 3 months and you will be very happy.

Educate, Don't Sell

Much has been written about the rise of the millennial consumer. The buying power they are bringing to the market, and the way they want to purchase, are powerful trends that we need to be aware of. Maybe they aren't your ideal target consumer, but they are such a force in the marketplace that they can't be ignored. One of their main desires is to make their own decision to purchase, rather than being sold to. They have a huge desire for information, research, social proof, and background information before they make a purchase. This is a good business practice for all situations. Not everyone *requires* this approach, but nearly all will appreciate it. Educate rather than sell.

The amazing Gary Vee talks about this sequence "Jab, Jab, Jab, Left Hook". The business application for us is, "Give, Give, Give, Ask." Provide your ideal bullseye customers valuable, relevant educational content. Give them DIY (do it yourself) tips on home maintenance, seasonal checklists for all the mechanical systems in their home, cleaning and organizing ideas.

Then, when they do need your Handyman Service, they will naturally think of you, the thoughtful experts that helped them over the past several months. You will be the natural and obvious choice because of all the value you have given them.

Remember that providing educational content is a very nice thing to do, but it is also cementing your business and brand in the mind of that consumer as an expert. You want to be known as an expert, trusted advisor. You aren't a vendor or a salesperson, you are a trusted advisor. If people are reading your content and using the advice you give, they will naturally form a positive image of you and your brand. This makes it easy and natural for them to call on you for services when the time is right.

<u>They aren't ready now…</u>

Sometimes people will seek you out when they have an immediate need. When the car breaks down (again) people go out shopping for a car. They need a car now and they are ready to decide and a purchase. This is a wonderful thing when customers just walk in off the street, but our job in marketing is to make them walk into OUR car dealership when the need arises.

This means that we need to build a relationship of trust over time. When people begin to interact with our brand, the probably are *not* ready to purchase. They may not even know that they need a new car at the time they first encounter your business, but if you give valuable, interesting content, they will continue to follow and learn.

Marketing is a journey – a long term project that builds a tribe of raving fans who will think of you when the time is right. Don't be in a hurry. Most people aren't ready to change suppliers right away – the marketing content you provide allows them to learn from you and about you. Later, if their primary service provider makes a mistake, isn't available, or just fails to show them love and attention, they will be ready to give you a try. This is where marketing ends, and sales/customer service take over. Our job as marketers is to nurture this amazing tribe of future potential customers. Keep them engaged and interested. We want to be top of mind when they think of services in our industry. This takes time, patience, and consistency, but it is worth it.

The Marketing Hourglass – beyond the first sale

John Jantsch has a beautiful concept in his book, Duct Tape Marketing: The Marketing Hourglass. Many people talk about a marketing funnel – the wide opening at the top that catches many prospects and begins them on a customer journey with a few of them coming out the bottom of the funnel as customers. This funnel concept is great.

You won't ever sell to every person you begin talking to – there are too many things that change throughout the process. Every industry is different, but we can all agree that nobody closes 100% of the deals they pitch to a client. If you do, then you aren't making enough pitches!

The point Jantsch makes is that this is only half the customer journey. If you stop at this point, you are leaving massive value on the table. Yes, industries vary widely on timing and frequency of purchase. You only buy a home every 7 years (on average), but you might visit your favorite florist once per quarter. Still, even with big ticket, infrequent purchases, there is massive potential after the first sale. This is why we want the funnel to flare out again at the bottom – it becomes the source of raving fans, repeat business, and referrals.

KNOW, LIKE, TRUST, TRY, BUY, REPEAT, REFER

Nobody follows this linear journey in the same way. Some people skip steps, while others get hung up at a particular stage and never progress at all. Following the path precisely isn't important for one specific client, but this general flow should represent the journey of your entire customer base. This general direction gives you a way to spot where things are dropping off. Where do you lose people in the process? This is the stage you need to tighten up, improve, and monitor.

KNOW – this is the most basic awareness that your company and product exist. This can be done via social media, events, or print advertising.

LIKE – now they have a bit of a flavor for your brand and your offerings. Maybe they have heard your podcast or read your helpful email newsletters. You are on their radar as a potential service provider when the time is right.

TRUST – you are an expert and trusted advisor in their mind. All we are waiting for is the need to arise, and you will get your first sale. Depending on the industry, product, and investment level, this could take weeks or even years until the time is right.

TRY – to the extent you can, it is great to have some type of a 'starter package.' The client gets great value, and you get to demonstrate your expertise. This isn't a free sample or even a loss leader, but it isn't the fully customized deluxe package. Make it easy for them to pull out their wallet and make a purchase.

BUY – this is getting more serious. They have upgraded to a better, mainstream product. Instead of just buying Life Insurance from you, they are committing to a full financial plan. This requires much more trust and it locks them into your system.

REPEAT – again, every industry is different, but this is really where the money is for most companies. You have already done the hard work of getting them to make the first purchase, and now they are coming back for more. They are fans and they are really the lifeblood of your company. Treat these repeat buyers like gold. They are 'gold' for your long-term business success.

REFER – this is the holy grail. These are the people that get inside the red velvet rope first. They think enough of your products to risk some of their own social capital to refer a friend. This is so valuable that some businesses track and reward people for referrals. Incentives are a double-edged sword, so enter this plan carefully. However you get there, an honest referral to a friend is the highest compliment a business can receive.

The entire point of this section is not to stop at the first sale. If you sell capital equipment or real estate, your sales cycle may be very long, but don't give up after the first transaction. You are leaving massive opportunity on the table if you don't stay in touch and cultivate an ongoing relationship with the client after the sale.

Chapter 5 – Release the Brakes
Summary and Notes

Now that you have all the tools, it is just a matter of committing and sticking with it. Never, ever, ever give up!

Never put a hard sell on a new potential customer. Educate them and offer amazing value up front. Later, they will be coming back to you when it is time to buy. They come back on their timeline.

Also, don't ever stop after the first sale. Marketing is not a funnel, but rather an hourglass. Once people buy, they will be positioned to become a raving fan and bring more people to your business.

NOTES:

Chapter 6 – Go for It!

<u>Putting it All Together</u>

Armed with all this information, you are truly ready to begin. There is nothing holding you back except fear and procrastination. Don't hesitate – start today with one step, and then repeat tomorrow. Here is all you have learned:

Chapter 1 – Back to the Basics. Here we laid the foundation of Marketing as an ongoing series of activities to systematically promote your business. We discussed the difference between an unchanging vision and specific (sometimes temporary) tactics to execute on that vision. We also talked about the mindset required to Market on an ongoing basis to see results.

Chapter 2 – Let's Get Started. This is the real meat of the content. Clearly defining yourself (the business), the problem you solve, and the people you solve it for. Don't be afraid to be too narrow. The old saying is, "there are riches in the niches." Being a generalist is a disaster in many cases, so be selective and focus on the people you are called to serve. Others will come too, and that is just fine.

Chapter 3 – Setting the Foundation. With the discovery work above, you may have to adjust your brand image or your product offerings to align with your mission. This can be done over time without throwing away your existing clients. Small, intentional shifts over time will help you really thrive as an aligned business. Once you begin this journey, you will also distill your brand message into a Unique Selling Proposition (USP).

Chapter 4 – Do the Work. The final step is to determine where and how your ideal target customers want to hear from you.

Once you know where they hang out and where they search for experts in your field, it is time to execute. Review all the different specific tactics and pick a few that resonate with your customers (maybe not things *you* like best). This chapter closes with a call to action – "Just Do It." Don't let fear hold you back. Execute consistently.

Chapter 5 – Release the Brakes. Here we reinforced that this is a long-term process, not a blowout sale for the weekend. We describe the customer journey and recognize that potential clients are in different places along the path. Patient and consistent communication, with valuable educational content – these are the keys.

That's it! If you have diligently followed this process and done the exercises with intent, you can transform your business. Consistent action is the only missing ingredient, but you can't continue down the path blindly.

Measure, Tweak, Repeat

On a regular, but *infrequent* basis, you need to measure and review each of your tactics. Their effectiveness may not be what you hoped, your market may shift, or specific tactics may fall out of favor in general. You can't blindly decide that your marketing will be weekly social posts and monthly email blasts and then never evaluate this choice again. Every part of business needs to be evaluated, tweaked, and improved over time.

Everything Works A Little. We fully believe that is true, but not every*thing* works as effectively as every other thing in all markets, industries, and specific businesses. Your time is limited, and most likely Marketing isn't your full-time job. You have to be smart and strategic. You need to focus on the high value activities that really bring the best results. Results may be subjective – maybe it is social followers, new inquiries about your product, or actual sales. Sales and profits are the ultimate measuring stick of success, but all the marketing activities ahead of the sale are still critically important, even if they don't directly result in a sale today. Be mindful of how you will measure success in each specific tactic/channel.

Sadly, the problem with most small business owners that take on the Marketing role is not that they are too committed and consistent. Instead, it is the opposite. They get bored, busy, or frustrated with no immediate results. The chances of your going *too long* with a particular campaign isn't usually the danger area, but it is still worth mentioning. If you aren't quite sure, you probably need to stay the course another 30-60 days. Then, with sufficient experience and data, make an honest evaluation and pivot specific tactics as needed.

Final Thoughts

Marketing has been the most rewarding, interesting part of running a small business the past 23 years. I am blessed to have a wonderful partner in the business, but she always let me take the lead on marketing. Nothing I have done has been in a vacuum, and the success is certainly not mine alone. 'Everything Works A Little' doesn't just apply to marketing activities. *Everything* in your business must be rowing in the same direction. All the pieces have to work together for the entire machine to thrive. Pricing, product, and people. All these working together for the greater good will result in Profit – the final 'P' and the ultimate measure of business financial success.

Rose City Label has been an amazing Marketing laboratory to test theories and learn. I am also very curious about business and marketing and read about these topics constantly. There is a suggested book list attached. Since we really started taking Marketing seriously and intentionally focused on it, our business has more than doubled. That is over about a 12-year period, and those 12 years were years 82-94 of the business! We were an established and respected company in our industry, but kind of stuck at a specific level. Now, we have broken through that ceiling and continue to thrive. It hasn't been without setbacks – 3 years ago we lost our biggest, most important client to a larger, lower-cost national competitor. That hurt, but with hard work we have replaced all that revenue and are in sight of another record year.

Finally, massive amounts of the credit for our success goes to our team. My sister and I are privileged to lead an amazing team of women and men that do the hard work every day. We try to lead well and value them, but I am still very thankful for their efforts.

This book has been percolating inside of me for years, and the first words were written over 5 years ago. I am thankful for gentle nudges from mentors and friends at the right time to finish it and share it with you. Thank you for reading. If you learned anything positive and useful, please pass the book along to someone else who can use it. More importantly, the greatest thanks I could ever receive would be your implementation and benefitting from these ideas. That is the purpose of this project – to make small business marketing accessible for everyone. So, before you put this book down, commit to taking one step forward. You got this!

With Gratitude and Humility,

Scott Pillsbury
Portland, OR
May 20, 2021

Chapter 6 – Go For It!
Summary and Notes

If you have made it this far, you have everything you need to move your business forward with consistent marketing actions. The only thing you need to do now, is act.

What will you commit to? What is the next right action?

COMMITMENT THIS WEEK:
_____
_____
_____
_____
_____
_____

COMMITMENT THIS QUARTER:
_____
_____
_____
_____
_____
_____
_____
_____
_____
_____

Recommended Reading List

Throughout my career I have refined, combined, and improved many business ideas. I have customized ideas to fit my situation – and you will too. But there are no new ideas. Everything Works a Little is just a compilation of great ideas I got from other people. Like everyone, I have had success because I have stood on the shoulders of giants. I feel fortunate to have access to all these books, as well as courses, videos, friends, and mentors that have given me key ideas over the years. I have over 100 business books in my personal library and I continue to add to it every month. There is no end to learning. If you get just *one* good idea from a book, it is worth the $20 and the few hours it takes to read it. If that idea isn't worth it to you, then you aren't applying the concepts. This is a very small selection of the most important books that helped me along the way.

Duct Tape Marketing by John Jantsch. This is the book that started it all for me back in 2009. The techniques in the book may be a bit dated, but the concepts are golden.

Book Yourself Solid by Michael Port. Narrow your target audience, and then cut it again. The red velvet rope concept comes from this book. Always narrow your focus.

The E-Myth by Michael Gerber. Absolutely critical insights about working *on* the business rather than *in* the business. Being a great plumber doesn't mean you can run a plumbing business successfully. They are entirely different skill sets.

Traction by Geno Wickman. This is an overall operation manual for your small business. It is not marketing focused but is a great resource for running an excellent business.

The One Thing by Gary Keller. This helps you focus very tightly on the very most important thing, rather than diverting attention to other, less important things.

The Compound Effect by Darren Hardy. Small changes, done consistently, make a huge difference. Don't be overwhelmed. Start small, act, then do it again tomorrow.

Deep Work by Cal Newport. It is essential that we block our time for meaningful, planned work to advance our business and not fall victim to the ringing phone.

The 12 Week Year by Brian Moran. Beautiful framework to set quarterly (12-week goals) to stay focused and make massive progress. One year is a very long time to focus.

Atomic Habits by James Clear. Again, this is more personal productivity, but it is helpful as you build the habit of marketing your business consistently.

About the Author

Scott Pillsbury grew up in Portland, Oregon. He has always been fascinated with technology, business, and how things work. He was lucky to have a Father with high standards, but also a total belief that anything is possible. His Father Mike was an entrepreneur and free-spirited individual with an infectious smile. He passed way too early, but his mentorship and spirit live on in Scott and his sister, and in Rose City Label.

Scott graduated from the U.S. Air Force Academy, earning a B.S. in Management with a Japanese language minor. More than the academics, he learned leadership, discipline, and made lifelong friends. All these things have helped him in business and in life.

Outside of work, Scott enjoys fitness, travel, snow and water skiing, and martial arts.

For more information, visit our website at
www.everythingworksalittle.com

www.ingramcontent.com/pod-product-compliance
Lightning Source LLC
Chambersburg PA
CBHW070130230526
45472CB00004B/1499